JOSH ALLEN

Making a Difference Through Football

By Katie Kawa

KidHaven PUBLISHING

People Who Make a Difference

Published in 2024 by
KidHaven Publishing, an Imprint of Greenhaven Publishing, LLC
2544 Clinton St.
Buffalo, NY 14224

Designer: Deanna Paternostro
Editor: Katie Kawa

Photo credits: Cover, pp. 5, 11, 20 Steve Jacobson/Shutterstock.com; p. 7 (main) Kevin Sabitus/AP Photo; p. 7 (inset) Danita Delimont/Shutterstock.com; p. 9 Debby Wong/Shutterstock.com; p. 13 Kirby Lee/Alamy Stock Photo; p. 15 Joshua Bessex/AP Photo; p. 17 All-Pro Reels/Flickr.com; p. 18 Matt Rourke/AP Photo; p. 21 T.Sumaetho/Shutterstock.com.

Library of Congress Cataloging-in-Publication Data

Names: Kawa, Katie, author.
Title: Josh Allen : making a difference through football / Katie Kawa.
Description: Buffalo, New York : KidHaven Publishing, [2024] | Series: People who make a difference | Includes bibliographical references and index.
Identifiers: LCCN 2023010385 | ISBN 9781534544352 (library binding) | ISBN 9781534544345 (paperback) | ISBN 9781534544369 (ebook)
Subjects: LCSH: Allen, Josh, 1996–Juvenile literature. | Buffalo Bills (Football team)–Juvenile literature. | Quarterbacks (Football)–Biography–Juvenile literature. | Football players–United States–Biography–Juvenile literature.
Classification: LCC GV939.A534 K38 2024 | DDC 796.33092 [B]–dc23/eng/20230308
LC record available at https://lccn.loc.gov/2023010385

Printed in the United States of America

Some of the images in this book illustrate individuals who are models. The depictions do not imply actual situations or events.

CPSIA compliance information: Batch #CSKH24: For further information contact Greenhaven Publishing LLC at 1-844-317-7404.

CONTENTS

LEADING HIS TEAM

A quarterback is often seen as one of the leaders on a football team, and that matters a lot to Josh Allen. He works hard to lead his team—the Buffalo Bills—to big wins on the field. He also works hard to be a leader in his community when he's not throwing touchdowns or leaping over players from the other team.

Josh takes his role, or job, as a leader **seriously**. He believes it's his job to help people—from helping his teammates succeed to helping sick kids feel better—and he has fun doing it!

In His Words

"I feel I'm the same person off the field as I am on the field."

— Interview with the Buffalo Bills website from July 2019

Josh has become a star in the National Football League (NFL) for what he does on and off the field. He makes a difference everywhere he goes!

ON THE FARM

Josh Allen's path to becoming an NFL superstar started on a farm very far from his future home in Buffalo, New York. He was born on May 21, 1996, in Firebaugh, California. Josh's family owned a farm where they grew crops such as cotton, cantaloupe, and wheat.

Josh helped out around the farm with his brother and two sisters, and he played football in school. He learned what it meant to lead a team as the quarterback of the Firebaugh High School Eagles. Josh finished high school in 2014, but he wasn't finished playing football.

In His Words

"Seeing my dad wake up super early when the sun wasn't even out and then coming home when the sun was set, he worked his tail off to provide for our family and did a great job. He's the most selfless man I know, and I think if I'm half the man he is, I'll be all right in this world."

— Interview with ESPN from December 2017

Firebaugh, California

Life in Buffalo (above) isn't like life in Firebaugh! However, Josh still keeps his hometown team close to his heart. In 2021, Josh teamed up with Bills fans—known as Bills Mafia—to raise money for Firebaugh High School. They raised $100,000!

FINDING HIS PLACE

Josh wanted to play football in college, but he didn't get any offers to play for a major school. Instead, he first played for Reedley College, which is a **junior college**. After having some success at Reedley College—and going through a **growth spurt**—he continued playing football at the University of Wyoming. He started school there in 2015.

Josh played well enough at Wyoming to be chosen in the 2018 NFL draft. The draft is an event where NFL teams choose which college players will join their team. Josh was chosen in the first round by the Buffalo Bills.

In His Words

"I was a no star, no offer guy out of high school. I sent emails every day to almost every coach in the nation … All I was asking for was an opportunity."

— Interview with ESPN from 2017

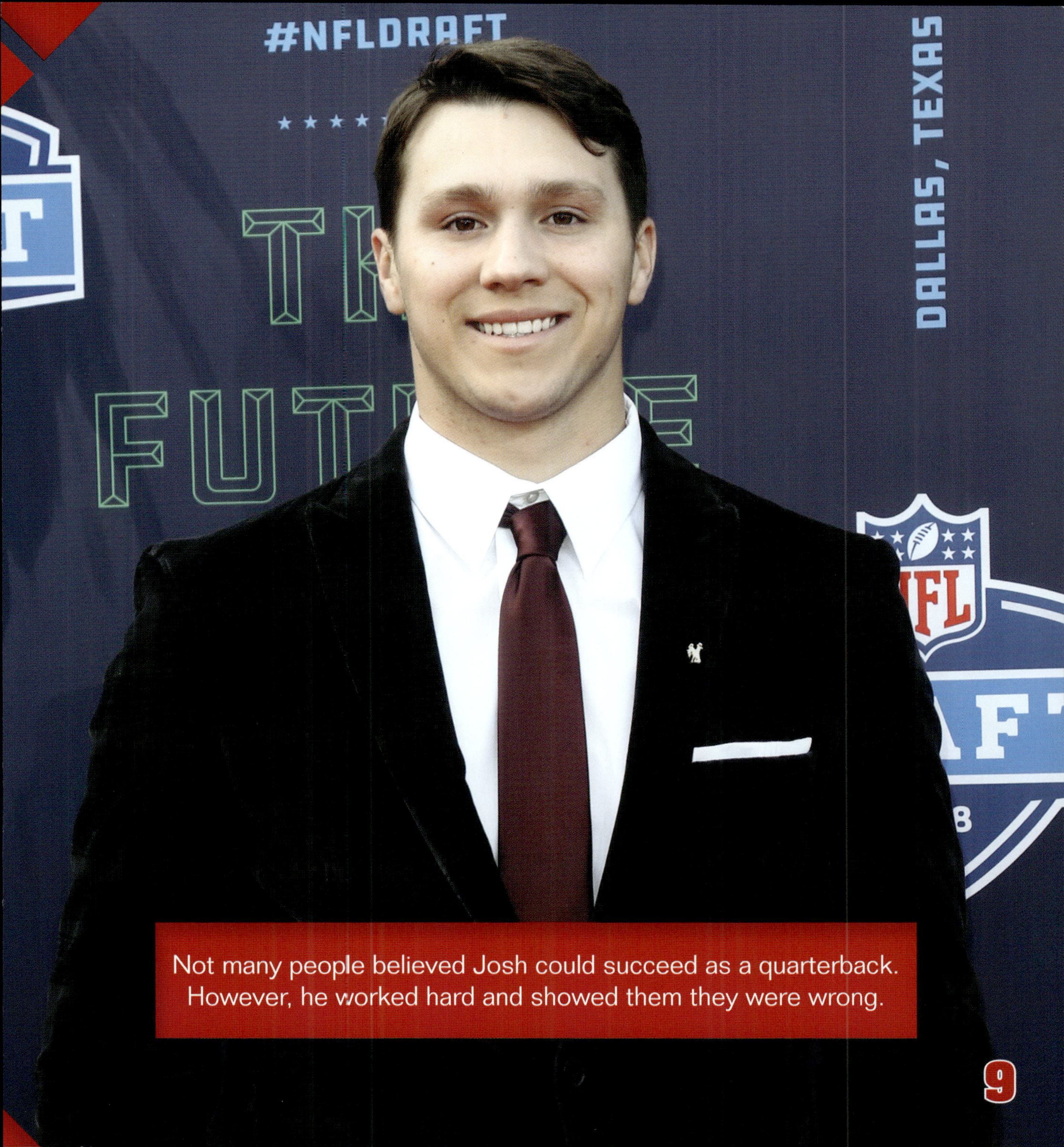

Not many people believed Josh could succeed as a quarterback. However, he worked hard and showed them they were wrong.

MAKING THE PLAYOFFS

Josh Allen played his first game for the Buffalo Bills in 2018. He helped turn the Bills from a team that was known for not making the **playoffs** to a team that's often thought of as one of the best in the NFL.

Josh helped lead the Bills to the playoffs in 2020. The next year, he helped them get all the way to the **AFC Championship** game. In 2022, Josh was the quarterback during the NFL's first "perfect game" when the Bills scored on every **drive** against the New England Patriots during the playoffs.

In His Words

"If you didn't want to believe in me, that's OK, because I'll make a believer out of you."

— Interview with the Denver Post from June 2017

The Bills played in the playoffs again in 2023. Josh has gained a lot of fans for his exciting plays in both the regular season—the time before the playoffs—and the postseason.

A TEAM PLAYER

Josh is known for being a good teammate. He's said he wants the people he plays with to know he cares about them. He works hard every game to show them he'll do whatever it takes to help them win. He also supports his teammates when they're raising money for a cause that's important to them.

Josh is honest about the times when he could have played better. He believes being a good leader means taking **responsibility** for how his team plays, especially after hard losses. It also means shining the spotlight on his teammates when they do something great.

In His Words

"I want to help my teammates in whatever way possible on and off the field."

— Interview with the Buffalo Bills website from July 2019

Josh has special handshakes with many of his teammates. He said he likes doing them to show his teammates he **appreciates** them.

HELPING KIDS

Josh believes it's just as important to make a difference off the football field as it is to make a difference on it. He's chosen to work hard to make a difference in the lives of kids who are very sick.

Josh first began visiting sick kids in Buffalo during his rookie, or first, year with the Bills. He's continued to spend time at John R. Oishei Children's Hospital in Buffalo ever since. He even talked to sick kids **virtually** when he couldn't visit the hospital during the **COVID-19 pandemic**.

In His Words

"As a rookie I did a few visits to see some kids … And when I did these visits, I just realized how easily I could make an impact [difference] on someone and just brighten their day by showing up and being there to show them that people care."

— Interview with the *Bleacher Report* website from November 2022

Josh knows he has a lot of young fans. He likes to make them happy however he can, including taking pictures with them, giving them signed footballs or other gear, and spending time with them when they're in the hospital.

HONORING HIS GRANDMOTHER

Oishei Children's Hospital is a place that means a lot to Josh. Bills fans know this, so they knew exactly where to give money in honor of Josh's grandmother, Patricia. She died the day before Josh helped the Bills score 44 points in a win over the Seattle Seahawks in 2020.

With the money fans gave, Josh and his family started the Patricia Allen Fund. It supports the hospital in many ways. For example, money from the fund was used to create the Patricia Allen Pediatric Recovery Wing in 2021. This space in the hospital includes a play area called the Bills Fans Fun Zone.

In His Words

"The [care] that the staff at Oishei shows families and patients during their time in the hospital absolutely exemplifies [shows] what it means to live in the city of good neighbors here in Buffalo."

— Speech given after a tour of the Patricia Allen Pediatric Recovery Wing of John R. Oishei Children's Hospital in November 2021

Bills Mafia is known for raising money for good causes, including the Patricia Allen Fund. Many of them gave $17 to Oishei Children's Hospital because Josh wears number 17. By the end of 2020, Josh and his fans had raised more than $1 million!

A COMMUNITY HEALS

Josh has also helped the Buffalo community in other ways. On May 14, 2022, a man killed 10 people in a mass shooting at a grocery store in Buffalo. It was a **racist** attack on Black people in the city, and the people of Buffalo were left feeling sad and afraid.

Josh and his teammates wanted to help. They visited the store where the shooting took place and comforted people there. They brought flowers to honor those who'd died, and they served food to the people who came to see them.

In His Words

"Going around, giving hugs to people, taking pictures with people, trying to put a smile on their face … That warms my heart—knowing that we do make a difference."

— Interview after visiting the site of the Buffalo mass shooting in May 2022

The Life of Josh Allen

1996
Josh is born on May 21 in Firebaugh, California.

2014
Josh finishes high school and plays football for Reedley College.

2015
Josh starts school at the University of Wyoming.

2018
Josh is drafted by the Buffalo Bills and plays in his first NFL game.

2020
Josh plays in his first NFL playoff game and works with his family to start the Patricia Allen Fund.

2021
The Bills reach the AFC Championship game, and the Patricia Allen Pediatric Recovery Wing is built at John R. Oishei Children's Hospital.

2022
Josh plays in a "perfect" playoff game against the New England Patriots, helps the Buffalo community heal from a mass shooting in May, and plays golf in The Match to raise money to help others.

2023
The Bills make the playoffs for the fourth year in a row with Josh as quarterback.

Josh hasn't been playing in the NFL for very long, but he's already made a big difference on the football field and off of it.

SPREADING SMILES

Josh knows he's one of the most famous faces in the NFL, and he uses his fame for good. He's sold coffee, cereal, and other things with his name and face on them to raise money for Oishei Children's Hospital. He also took part in The Match—a 2022 golf event in which NFL quarterbacks teamed up against each other to raise money for important causes.

Josh Allen works hard, but he also likes to have fun. Making his teammates, his fans, and sick kids smile is one of the biggest ways he makes a difference!

In His Words

"One thing I'm always going to have is a positive attitude and if you want to say I'm 'happy go lucky,' that's okay with me."

— Interview with the Buffalo Bills website from July 2019

Be Like Josh Allen!

Believe in yourself, and support your friends so they can believe in themselves too.

If you make a mistake, take responsibility for it.

Try to have a positive attitude, or way of thinking and acting.

Raise money for groups that help sick kids.

Be a leader on a sports team, in student government, or in a club.

If you have a goal, work hard to reach it.

Show and tell your friends you care about them.

If someone you know is sick, call or visit them.

If you know someone who's going through a hard time, tell them you're there for whatever they need, and ask if they'd like a hug.

You don't have to be a quarterback to be like Josh Allen. Anyone can be a leader and someone who helps out in their community!

GLOSSARY

AFC Championship: A contest held every year to decide which is the best team in the American Football Conference (AFC)—a group made up of half the teams in the National Football League (NFL).

appreciate: To value and be thankful for something.

COVID-19 pandemic: An event that began in China in 2019 in which a disease that causes breathing problems, a fever, and other health issues spread rapidly around the world and made millions of people sick in a short period of time.

drive: A series of plays in which a football team's offense has the ball and is trying to score.

growth spurt: An occurrence of growing quickly and suddenly in a short period of time.

junior college: A school students can attend after high school that offers two years of studies.

playoffs: A series of games played after the regular season of a sport is over to find out who the best team is that season.

racist: Relating to the practice of treating others poorly because they are part of a different race, or group of people who look alike in certain ways.

responsibility: Something a person must take care of or be in charge of.

seriously: Done with care.

virtually: Done using a computer.

FOR MORE INFORMATION

WEBSITES

NFL.com: Josh Allen

www.nfl.com/players/josh-allen-4/

The NFL's official website has a page just for Josh Allen, featuring facts, news stories, and videos.

The Patricia Allen Fund

www.ochbuffalo.org/foundation/patricia-allen-fund/

The official website for the Patricia Allen Fund explains how the fund was started and the ways it's helping kids in Buffalo.

BOOKS

Anderson, Josh. *Buffalo Bills*. Parker, CO: The Child's World, 2022.

Coleman, Ted. *Josh Allen: Superstar Quarterback*. Mendota Heights, MN: Press Box Books, 2021.

Lowe, Alexander. *Josh Allen*. Minneapolis, MN: Lerner Publications, 2022.

INDEX